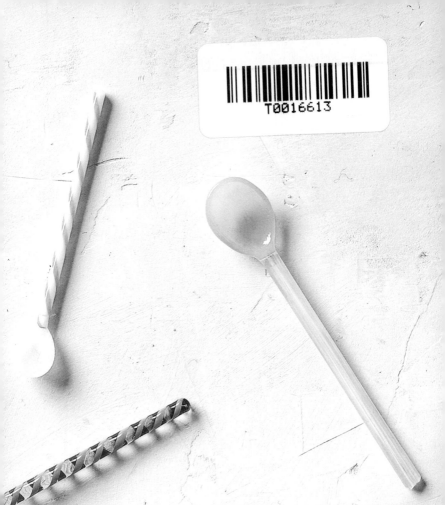

T0016613

Dessert Cocktails

Dessert Cocktails

40 DELICIOUSLY INDULGENT SWEET DRINKS

**DAVID T. SMITH
& KELI RIVERS**

Photography by
ALEX LUCK

RYLAND PETERS & SMALL
LONDON • NEW YORK

Senior designer Toni Kay
Production manager
  Gordana Simakovic
Editorial director Julia Charles
Creative director
  Leslie Harrington
Food stylist Lorna Brash
Prop stylist Luis Peral

Indexer Vanessa Bird

First published in 2022 by
Ryland Peters & Small
20–21 Jockey's Fields
London WC1R 4BW
and
341 E 116th Street
New York, 10029

www.rylandpeters.com

10 9 8 7 6 5 4 3 2 1

Text © David T. Smith & Keli Rivers
2022. Design and photographs
© Ryland Peters & Small 2022.

ISBN: 978-1-78879-435-0

A CIP record for this book is available
from the British Library.
US Library of Congress CIP data
has been applied for.

Printed in China

Author dedications:
To Queenie & Big T

*To Sally and Joshua, for not telling our
parents when I stole your holiday sweets.*

Contents

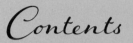

Introduction

Dessert cocktails occupy a unique space in the drinking world: often served at an occasion, after a rather satisfying meal, and accompanied by a feeling of indulgence and a touch of decadence. They are jubilant cocktails that are almost never consumed in sorrow or anger. They are also one of only a few types of drink that can easily replace an entire course at dinner.

Like other groups of drinks, such as Martinis or Old Fashioneds, dessert cocktails have experienced their fair share of peaks and troughs in popularity, including a golden era around and after Prohibition as sweeter and stronger flavours helped to cover up the underlying unrefined flavours of bootleg booze. After the Second World War, tastes moved towards dryer cocktails, before a return to fun and fruitiness in the sixties and seventies. Around the start of the new millennium, interest piqued again and the Porn Star Martini was added to the cocktail canon (or should that be sweet trolley?).

Recent years have seen renewed interest in dessert cocktails. The Porn Star Martini was followed by the Espresso Martini in being named one of the most popular cocktails of the year.

This book seeks to take you on a journey to explore a whole range of delicious dessert cocktails. We have endeavoured to embrace a wide range of styles of drink – big and small, strong and long, hot and cold – as well as utilizing a good assortment of spirits and liqueurs.

The first chapter presents classic dessert cocktails: exploring old-school favourites and the stories behind them, including the White Russian, Grasshopper and the Alexander, as well as lesser-known historical recipes that time has since forgotten. The contemporary chapter brings dessert cocktails up to the present day with blended slushie cocktails, those inspired by the ice cream parlour, and even one that uses breakfast cereal as a garnish. The recipes in the experimental chapter has been particularly inspired by dessert dishes that people know and love such as black forest gateau, banoffee pie and rhubarb and custard. And finally, we bring you a selection of recipes for special occasions: with a drink for every season, as well as Valentine's Day, Burns' Night and the Christmas holiday season.

Lots of these cocktail recipes contain milk, cream, or other dairy products, but the recipes have been specifically created so that they also work well with non-dairy alternatives such as oat milk and cream. The recipes themselves are just a guide and will hopefully provide a template for you to create your very own customizations and creations to enjoy at home.

Classic

Gin pearl

Ice cream is not necessarily the first mixer you think of for gin, but the combination of the two has been enjoyed for nearly a century - the inspiration for the following cocktail goes back to 1927. The drink is rich and indulgent, but balanced, and the really exciting thing is that the flavour is limited only by the varieties of ice cream you can find!

45 ml/1½ oz. gin
1 scoop (approx 50 g/2 oz.)
    ice cream of your choice
    (vanilla, chocolate or
    strawberry are great
    ones to start with)
garnish of your choice
    (to complement the
    ice cream flavour)

SERVES 1

Add the ingredients to a cocktail shaker and shake vigorously without ice and strain into a coupe glass. Garnish with the decoration of your choice.

Variation: For an extra treat, add a splash (10–15 ml/2 tsp–½ oz.) of chilled sparkling wine to the drink after pouring.

White Russian

The White Russian is a cult drink if ever there was one, largely due to its popularity with "The Dude" in the film *The Big Lebowski*. Created to help sell a coffee liqueur by Southern Comfort in 1965, the White Russian is a take on the 1950s cocktail the Black Russian. For a longer drink, add the ingredients to a Collins glass and top up with cola to make a Colorado Bulldog.

60 ml/2 oz. vodka
30 ml/1 oz. coffee liqueur
(such as Conker Cold Brew)
a splash of double/heavy
cream

SERVES 1

Add the vodka and coffee liqueur to a rocks glass or tumbler along with ice cubes, then pour over the cream. Serve the drink at once with a stirrer to allow the drinker to mix at their pleasure.

Mudslide

Here, for extra indulgence, the cream is replaced with Irish cream liqueur, adding richness and gentle spice.

25 g/1 oz. melted dark
chocolate and chocolate
shavings, to serve
30 ml/1 oz. vodka
30 ml/1 oz. coffee liqueur
45 ml/1½ oz. Irish cream liqueur

SERVES 1

Drizzle melted chocolate inside the rim of a rocks glass. Mix and serve the drink as for the White Russian (above), substituting the cream for Irish cream liqueur.

Three drinks all based on a mix of vodka, coffee and cream, but each with their own unique style.

Pink squirrel

A creation from the 1940s, this drink gained national attention in June 1951 when one newspaper headline declared "Shocking Pink Squirrel Wreaks Havoc in Bars", though most likely a PR stunt employed by Bols, makers of both liqueurs used in the cocktail.

30 ml/1 oz. crème de noyaux
30 ml/1 oz. white crème de cacao
45 ml/1½ oz. double/heavy cream
pink sugar, for the rim of the glass (optional)

SERVES 1

Coat the rim of a coupe glass with pink sugar (if using). Add the ingredients to a cocktail shaker with ice cubes and shake vigorously. Strain into the sugar-rimmed glass and serve at once.

Grasshopper

Eye-catching, indulgent and delightful... For a dryer drink, substitute the cream with vodka to create a Flying Grasshopper.

30 ml/1 oz. green crème de menthe
30 ml/1 oz. white crème de cacao
30 ml/1 oz. double/heavy cream
chocolate shavings, to garnish

SERVES 1

Add the ingredients to a cocktail shaker with ice cubes and shake vigorously. Strain into a coupe glass, garnish with chocolate shavings and serve at once.

Alexander

The Alexander was originally a gin-based drink, designed by Troy Alexander for a dinner celebrating the fictional character Phoebe Snow. The drink had to be pure white to reflect Phoebe's pristine dress.

The gin was later replaced with brandy to create the Alexander #2, which ultimately came to be more widely known as the Brandy Alexander. If you are feeling adventurous, you can substitute the gin here for bourbon, rum or even a blanco tequila!

45 ml/1½ oz. gin (or brandy
   for a Brandy Alexander)
30 ml/1 oz. white crème
   de cacao
15 ml/½ oz. double/
   heavy cream
freshly grated nutmeg,
   to garnish

SERVES 1

Add the ingredients to a cocktail shaker with ice cubes and shake vigorously. Strain into a cocktail glass. Garnish with a dusting of grated nutmeg and serve at once.

Espresso martini

Bartender-meets-barista with this coffee drink created by the late, great Dick Bradsell in London in the vodka-loving 1980s. The number of espresso beans is specific: according to ancient superstition, odd numbers are lucky!

45 ml/1½ oz. vodka or gin
15 ml/½ oz. coffee liqueur
**30 ml/1 oz. freshly made
  espresso coffee**
10 ml/2 tsp sugar syrup
3 espresso beans, to garnish

SERVES 1

Add the ingredients to a cocktail shaker with ice cubes and shake vigorously. Strain into a martini glass. Garnish by floating three coffee beans on the surface of the drink. Serve at once.

Stinger

The Stinger is a cocktail from the early 20th century that was, according to legend, popular with early aviators. It combines two components of traditional, after-dinner ceremony: the post-meal brandy and a wafer-thin after dinner chocolate mint.

60 ml/2 oz. brandy
25 ml/1 oz. white crème
    de menthe
mint sprig or chilled after
    dinner mint, to garnish

SERVES 1

Add the ingredients to a cocktail shaker with ice cubes and shake vigorously. Strain into an ice-filled tumbler or rocks glass. Garnish with a mint sprig or after dinner mint and serve at once.

Snowball

A simple but satisfying serve that is now seen as the epitome of Christmas drinking, but when it first appeared in the mid 1960s, it was actually enjoyed year-round. It has a light, refreshing quality with a zing of citrus – a drink for all seasons!

35 ml/1¼ oz. Advocaat
10 ml/2 tsp lime cordial (optional)
120 ml/4 oz. sparkling lemonade/lemon soda
lime slice and a cocktail cherry, to garnish

SERVES 1

Add the Advocaat and lime cordial (if using) to a highball glass filled with ice. Top up with lemonade. Garnish with a slice of lime and a cocktail cherry.

Contemporary

Miami vice

When you can't decide between two classic rum cocktails, why not combine them? This delicious frozen cocktail consists of two layers: one with the pineapple and coconut creaminess of a Piña Colada, and the other with the strawberry and lime zing of a Daiquiri.

1 x 250-ml/8½-oz. can premixed Strawberry Daiquiri
1 x 250-ml/8½-oz. can premixed Piña Colada
30 ml/1 oz. white rum

SERVES 2

Blend the Strawberry Daiquiri with ice and half of the white rum (15 ml/½ oz.) until it forms a smooth slush. Pour into a hurricane glass. Next, blend the Piña Colada with ice and the rest of the rum (15 ml/½ oz.). Pour into the same hurricane glass on top of the Strawberry Daiquiri slush, creating a layering effect. Serve at once with a straw.

Note: If you prefer, you can make the Piña Colada and Strawberry Daiquiri from scratch using your preferred recipes and then blend them.

EZ like Sunday morning

A dessert cocktail for a luxurious brunch, designed to be reminiscent of an orange creamsicle ice lolly. A lovely accompaniment to French toast, eggs Benedict, huevos rancheros or your usual Sunday morning treat.

20 ml/1 oz. Licor 43 liqueur (see page 58)
15 ml/½ oz. orange liqueur (such as Cointreau)
1 scoop vanilla ice cream
120 ml/4 oz. orange soda
whipped cream, to serve
brûléed orange slice, to garnish

SERVES 1

Add the liqueurs and ice cream to a sundae glass and top up with the orange soda. Garnish with whipped cream and the brûléed orange slice. Serve with both a spoon and a straw.

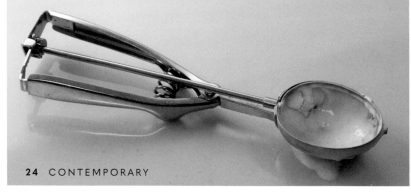

Something blue

A tropical tipple with both an exotic fruitiness and a sweet nuttiness; its alluring colour transporting you to the shoreline of a sun-kissed island, the sea lapping upon the golden sands

30 ml/1 oz. coconut rum
25 ml/¾ oz. vanilla vodka
45 ml/1½ oz. pineapple
   juice
10 ml/2 tsp Amaretto
15 ml/½ oz. lime juice
a float (approx. 10 ml/2 tsp)
   of blue Curaçao
pineapple wedges,
   to garnish

SERVES 1

Add the ingredients, apart from the blue Curaçao, to a cocktail shaker with ice cubes and shake vigorously. Pour into an ice-filled hurricane glass, or similar. Pour 10 ml/2 tsp blue Curaçao down the inside of the glass. The Curaçao will sink, creating the layered effect. Garnish with pineapple wedges and serve at once.

Fruit loop old fashioned

Created by Joseph Biolatto whilst working at Le Forvm bar in Paris. It differs from a typical Old Fashioned in two ways: the use of maple syrup to add sweetness, which is a lovely complement to the bourbon, and the unusual and rather colourful cereal garnish.

**60 ml/2 oz. bourbon
(such as Maker's Mark)
5–10 ml/1–2 tsp maple
syrup, to taste
3 dashes orange bitters
fruit-flavoured cereal hoops
(such as Froot Loops),
to garnish**

SERVES 1

Add the ingredients to a mixing glass with ice cubes and stir. Strain into a chilled tumbler or rocks glass over ice cubes and garnish with the colourful cereal. Serve at once.

Porn star martini

Invented by Douglas Ankrah of LAB Bar in London in 2002, this drink was designed to be stylish, confident, and fun. The dryness of the Champagne is a brilliant companion to the sweeter fruitiness of the drink.

60 ml/2 oz. vodka
15 ml/½ oz. passion fruit
   purée or Passoa liqueur
15 ml/½ oz. vanilla syrup
15 ml/½ oz. lime juice
½ passion fruit, to garnish
a shot glass of chilled
   Champagne (or other
   sparkling wine), to serve

SERVES 1

Add the ingredients (except the Champagne) to a cocktail shaker with ice cubes and shake vigorously. Strain into a coupe glass. Garnish with the passion fruit and serve at once with a shot glass of Champagne on the side.

Golden Cadillac

The retro revival inspired Golden Cadillac is served at Poor Red's BBQ restaurant in Northern California. It is said to have been created for a newly engaged couple who named it after their car.

30 ml/1½ oz. Galliano
30 ml/1½ oz. crème de cacao
20 ml/1 oz. single/light cream
chocolate shavings, to garnish

SERVES 1

Add the ingredients to a cocktail shaker with ice cubes and shake vigorously. Strain into a cocktail glass. Garnish with chocolate shavings and serve at once.

Graham cracker crunch

A sweet and spicy cocktail designed to emulate the classic American snack. RumChata is a rum-based, cream liqueur flavoured with cinnamon and baking spices.

20 ml/1 oz. RumChata
cream liqueur
20 ml/1 oz. blanco tequila
20 ml/1 oz. cinnamon whiskey
cinnamon and sugar, for the rim
of the glass and to garnish
(optional)

SERVES 1

Coat the rim of a cocktail glass with cinnamon sugar (if using). Add the ingredients to a cocktail shaker with ice cubes and shake vigorously. Strain into the sugar-rimmed glass. Sprinkle with a little extra cinnamon and serve at once.

Hot buttered fernet

Fernet-Branca is an Italian amaro well known for its bittersweet qualities, but in this drink it is far more accessible as a part of a cosy, warming cocktail that will transport you to an Alpine ski lodge.

45 ml/1½ oz. Fernet-Branca
15 ml/½ oz. Bénédictine
15 ml/½ oz. bourbon
120 ml/4 oz. hot water
½ tsp good-quality butter
   (ideally salted)
cinnamon stick and orange
   zest, to garnish

SERVES 1

Add the Fernet-Branca, Bénédictine and bourbon to a heatproof glass and top up with the hot water. Add the butter and stir until dissolved. Garnish with a cinnamon stick and an orange zest and serve at once.

Experimental

Rhubarb and custard old fashioned

The perfect combination of an old-fashioned candy and an old-fashioned cocktail, this brings back memories of old-time sweet shops.

45 ml/1½ oz. rhubarb gin
10 ml/2 tsp rhubarb cordial
   (rhubarb and ginger
   would also work)
20 ml/²⁄₃ oz. Angostura bitters
30 ml/1 oz. cream soda
strips of rhubarb, to garnish
mini shortbread cookies,
   to serve (optional)

SERVES 1

Add the ingredients, apart from the cream soda, to a mixing glass with ice and stir. Strain into a tumbler or rocks glass over ice cubes and top up with cream soda. Garnish with strips of raw rhubarb and serve at once with mini shortbreads on the side (if using).

Black Forest gateau

A staple of the 70s dinner party, the Black Forest Gateau is back, this time in cocktail form. With a mix of brandy, coffee and chocolate it is a superb dessert-cum-digestif.

45 ml/1½ oz. brandy
30 ml/1 oz. chilled
   espresso coffee
5 ml/1 tsp Bénédictine
15 ml/½ oz. maraschino
   cherry liqueur
2 dashes orange bitters
cocktail cherry and
   chocolate shavings,
   to garnish

SERVES 1

Add the ingredients to a cocktail shaker with ice cubes and shake vigorously. Strain into a coupe glass. Garnish with a cocktail cherry and chocolate shavings and serve at once.

Caramel apple toddy

The toffee or caramel apple has been the adversary of teeth and dentists at many a carnival, fair or bonfire night; thankfully with this drink you're less likely to lose a tooth.

60 ml/2 oz. Calvados
120 ml/4 oz. freshly brewed
hot English breakfast tea
10 ml/2 tsp caramel syrup,
plus extra to garnish
whipped cream, apple
slices and cinnamon
stick, to garnish

SERVES 1

Add the ingredients to a heatproof glass and stir until the caramel syrup has dissolved. Garnish with whipped cream, apple slices, a cinnamon stick and extra syrup, and serve at once.

Banoffee xxx

This drink captures the classic banoffee pie combination of banana, caramel and cream that has delighted for decades.

½ ripe banana, plus extra
   sliced banana to garnish
45 ml/1½ oz. vanilla vodka
15 ml/½ oz. banana liqueur
10 ml/2 tsp caramel syrup
15 ml/½ oz. milk
whipped cream and grated
   chocolate, to garnish

SERVES 1

Muddle the banana in a cocktail shaker, then add the other ingredients. Shake vigorously with ice cubes and strain into a cocktail glass. Garnish with whipped cream, banana slices and grated chocolate. Serve at once.

Lemon meringue pie

Another winner from the sweet trolley in a small yet punchy form.

45 ml/1½ oz. gin
1 tbsp lemon curd
15 ml/½ oz. limoncello
crushed meringue, to garnish
   or see Variation to create
   a burnt topping (as
   pictured on page 1)

SERVES 1

Add the ingredients to a cocktail shaker with ice cubes. Shake vigorously and strain into a cocktail glass. Garnish with crushed meringue and serve at once.

Variation: To create a topping for 2 drinks, whip 1 egg white with 65 g/⅓ cup sugar until stiff. Spoon half on top of each drink. Use a chef's blowtorch to toast the peaks.

Cake it to the limit

A very easy drink to make that embraces both vibrant citrus and buttery hazelnut. Frangelico is an Italian noisette (hazelnut liqueur) and has a distinctive, monk-shaped bottle.

45 ml/1½ oz. citrus
   gin (such as Sipsmith
   Lemon Drizzle)
30 ml/1 oz. Frangelico
10 ml/2 tsp lemon juice
sugar, for the rim of
   the glass (optional)
lemon zest, to garnish

SERVES 1

Coat the rim of a cocktail glass with sugar (if using). Add the ingredients to a cocktail shaker with ice cubes and shake vigorously. Strain into the sugar-rimmed glass. Garnish with a thin piece of lemon zest and serve at once.

Smoky chai cocktail

This south of the border tipple is all about smoky spice: it has a mix of tequila and mezcal as well as the decadent aromatics of chai tea.

45 ml/1½ oz. tequila
10 ml/2 tsp mezcal
35 ml/1¼ oz. cold chai tea
15 ml/½ oz. oat milk
   (or milk of your choice)
10 ml/2 tsp vanilla syrup
3 green cardamom pods,
   to garnish (optional)

SERVES 1

Add the ingredients to a cocktail shaker with ice cubes and shake vigorously. Strain into a large coupe glass. Garnish with cardamom pods (if using) and serve at once.

Seasonal

Japanese Spring sling

This drink is inspired by the beautiful blossoms of Japanese trees such as Sakura, as well as the country's love of a whisky highball. The Japanese Spring Sling is a crisp, refreshing drink with a hint of jamminess.

4 frozen peach slices
(to be used in place
of ice cubes to serve)
45 ml/1½ oz. Japanese
whisky (such as Toki)
1 large tsp peach conserve
3 dashes Angostura bitters
chilled sparkling/soda
water, to top up (approx.
80–100 ml/2¾–3⅓ oz.)
mint leaves, to garnish

SERVES 1

Add the ingredients, except the frozen peach slices, to a cocktail shaker with ice cubes and shake vigorously. Strain into a highball glass filled with the frozen peach slices. Top up with sparkling/soda water and garnish with the mint leaves. Serve at once.

Cherry clafoutis

Inspired by the classic French dessert, the Cherry Clafoutis is an ideal romantic cocktail for Valentine's Day or a date night – why save it for one night a year!

45 ml/1½ oz. brandy
15 ml/½ oz. white
   chocolate liqueur
   (such as Dooley's)
10 ml/2 tsp maraschino
   cherry liqueur
10 ml/2 tsp Amaretto
cocktail cherry, to garnish
dusting of hibiscus tea,
   to garnish

SERVES 1

Add the ingredients to a cocktail shaker with ice cubes and shake vigorously. Strain into a cocktail glass or small coupe. Garnish with a cherry and a dusting of hibiscus tea, ideally sprinkled over a heart-shaped stencil. Serve at once.

En la playa

A lively mix of fruit and floral flavours, this bright, refreshing thirst-quencher is ideal for summer.

45 ml/1½ oz. tequila
20 ml/1 oz. peach schnapps
30 ml/1 oz. orange juice
30 ml/1 oz. pineapple juice
15 ml/½ oz. lime juice

15 ml/½ oz. Iced Hibiscus Tea (see recipe below)
cocktail cherry and pineapple wedges, to garnish

SERVES 1

Add the ingredients to a cocktail shaker with ice cubes. Shake vigorously and strain into a highball glass. Garnish with a cocktail cherry and pineapple wedges. Serve at once with a straw.

ICED HIBISCUS TEA

1 hibiscus tea bag
2–3 tsp sugar
200 ml/6¾ oz. boiling water

Add the tea bag, sugar and water to a heatproof jug/pitcher. Stir to dissolve the sugar. Leave to cool. This recipe makes more than you need for one drink, but it will store in the fridge for up to 1 week.

Pumpkin spice Spanish coffee

A dramatic, spiced version of a classic Spanish coffee with warming brandy, fragrant orange and comforting baking spices.

30 ml/1 oz. rum
  or brandy (100
  proof/50% ABV)
20 ml/²/₃ oz. orange
  liqueur (such as
  Grand Marnier)
30 ml/1 oz. oat milk
5–10 ml/1–2 tsp
  pumpkin spice syrup
90 ml/3 oz. hot
  espresso coffee

TO SERVE
lemon wedge, sugar
  and mixed spice, for
  the rim of the glass
orange wedge studded
  with cloves, to garnish
10 ml/2 tsp high ABV/
  proof rum or brandy,
  to set on fire
  (optional)

SERVES 1

Add the main drink ingredients to a heatproof jug/pitcher and stir together. Wet the rim of a warmed heatproof glass with a lemon wedge and roll in sugar and mixed spice. Pour the hot coffee cocktail mixture into the glass, garnish with the clove-studded orange wedge and serve at once.

Variation: If you want a bit of theatre, before pouring the drink into the glass add 10 ml/2 tsp of the high proof rum/brandy to the glass and light on fire, then carefully rotate the glass to caramelize the sugar rim whilst simultaneously sprinkling over the spice mix. To put out the fire, pour over the hot coffee cocktail.

Burns' night off

In the cold depths of January we honour the birthday of Scottish poet Robert Burns. This drink celebrates some of the flavours of Scotch whisky: honey and spice, and that most Scottish of fruits: the raspberry.

45 ml/1½ oz. blended Scotch whisky
20 ml/¾ oz. Drambuie
10 ml/2 tsp raspberry liqueur
freshly grated nutmeg and a
    raspberry, to garnish

SERVES 1

Add the ingredients to a cocktail shaker with ice cubes. Shake vigorously and strain into a cocktail glass. Garnish with grated nutmeg and a raspberry. Serve at once.

Variation: For a Red Hot Robbie, add the alcohol to a heatproof glass, then top up with 100 ml/3⅓ oz. hot water and stir.

Hot spiced whiskey apple crumble

Licor 43 is a fruit and herb flavoured Spanish liqueur, which is used to perfection in this warming drink. The hot mulled cloudy apple recipe is delicious in its own right so worth making a batch.

35 ml/1¼ oz. bourbon or whiskey
15–20 ml/½–⅔ oz. Licor 43
150 ml/5 oz. Hot Mulled Cloudy Apple
   (see recipe below)
whipped cream and toasted nuts, to garnish

SERVES 1

Add the ingredients to a heatproof glass and gently stir. Garnish with whipped cream and toasted nuts and serve.

HOT MULLED CLOUDY APPLE

2 cinnamon sticks
4 star anise
10 cloves
a pinch of salt
½ orange
1 litre/quart cloudy apple juice
1 vanilla pod/bean, split
   OR ¼ tsp vanilla extract

Combine the ingredients together in a saucepan over medium heat. Simmer for 20 minutes. Use a ladle to serve and try to avoid putting any of the spices in the glass. Use as directed above, or enjoy as a mocktail.

Hot gin-gerbread

The first ever recorded gin and food pairing was gin and gingerbread at the Whitstable Oyster Fair. This drink introduces hot tea to the combination of gin and ginger, lengthening it and helping to keep out the winter chill.

45 ml/1½ oz. gin
30 ml/1 oz. gingerbread syrup
   or ginger wine
120 ml/4 oz. freshly brewed
   hot black tea or hot water
whipped cream and candied
   ginger, to garnish
mini gingerbread man, to serve

SERVES 1

Add the main drink ingredients to a heatproof glass and stir together gently. Serve topped with whipped cream, candied ginger and a mini gingerbread man.

Variation: For a short, chilled cocktail named The Cushing, combine 50 ml/1⅔ oz. dry gin with 25 ml/¾ oz. ginger wine shake vigorously with ice cubes, strain into a cocktail glass and serve at once.

Grandpa McCord's eggnog

No drink encapsulates the American festive period more than Eggnog! The extra here effort is really worth it.

4 eggs, separated
170 g/6 oz. sugar, plus 2 tbsp
1 tsp ground nutmeg
1 tsp salt
1 tsp vanilla extract
120 ml/4 oz. spiced rum
120 ml/4 oz. brandy
120 ml/4 oz. bourbon
355 ml/12 oz. whole milk
235 ml/8 oz. double/heavy cream
freshly grated nutmeg and/or
   chocolate decoration, to garnish

SERVES 4–6

Whisk the egg yolks with the 170 g/ 6 oz. sugar until fluffy and pale yellow. Whisk in the nutmeg, salt and vanilla extract. Slowly stir in the rum, brandy and bourbon, followed by the milk and cream. In a separate bowl, whip the egg whites and 2 tbsp sugar to stiff peaks, then fold into the yolk mixture.

Serve in tumblers, garnished with grated nutmeg and/or a chocolate decoration.

Index

Acknowledgements

Our thanks go to J-Money Barber, The Gin Archive, The Gin Genies, Bernie Pamplin & Mr. Damo, Rosie The Bear, Dimple "All Things Drinks" Athavia, DW & JP Smith, Gin Magazine, Gin-Gin Miller, Bill Owens, Rupert Conker, Lucy Francis, Veronika "VK" Karlova, The Spirits Business, Tob Tob Gorn, Jules Nourney, Dot Awcock, Stupot Ceng, Aaron "AK" Knoll, The Mothership & Bramble Bar, Nicholas Cook, The Swig & Ramblers, Emma Stokes, Sean Harrison, Seb Hamilton-Mudge, Jon Hillgren, The James Bond Dossier, Clayton & Ali Hartley, Sarah Mitchell, Adam Smithson, Olivier Ward, The Hayman Family, Eric Zandona & Co., Benedict Marston, Dan Szor, Dr. Anne Brock, Stephen Gould, Maritza Rocha-Alvarez, Natasha Bahrami, Joseph Biolatto, Douglas Ankrah, Dick Bradsell. My Swans near and far, Zahra Bates, Michelle and Jim Rivers, Diamond Ken, Andrew Robinson, My always roommate Allison Webber, The Donkeys and their Burrito, Dawn Heidemann, Amanda Schuster, Joshua Richholt and the The Hotsy Totsy Crew.

We'd also like to thank our publisher, Julia Charles, designer Toni Kay, creative director Leslie Harrington, and the rest of the team at RPS who, once again, have been a treat to work with. Thanks also go to Alex Luck, Lorna Brash and Luis Peral for creating the beautiful photographs. Finally, a special thanks to Sara Smith, without whom the book would not be possible.